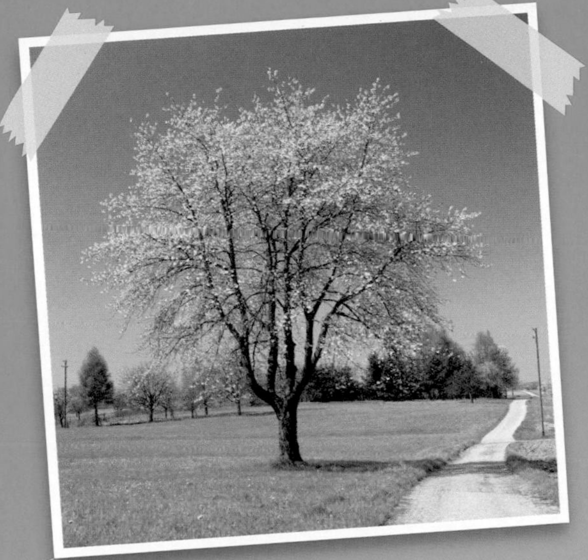

D0503794

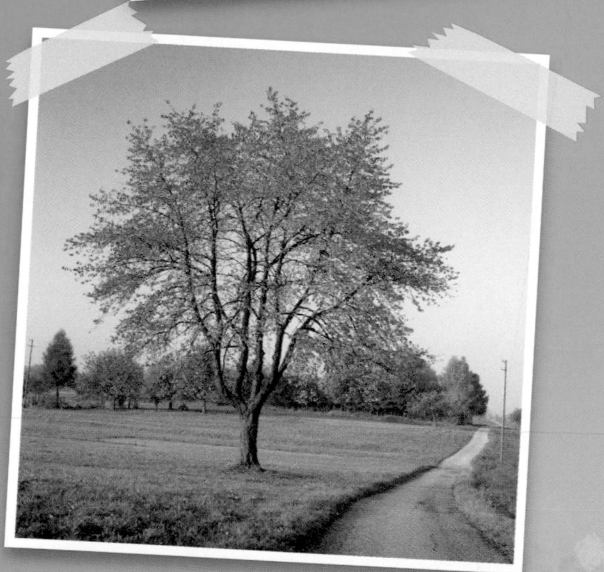

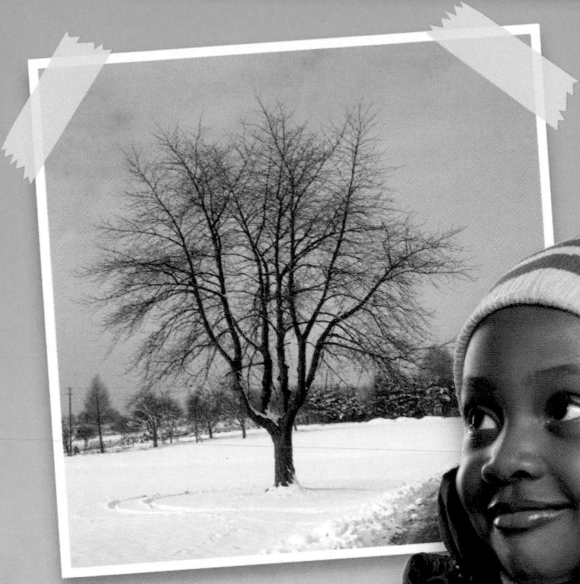

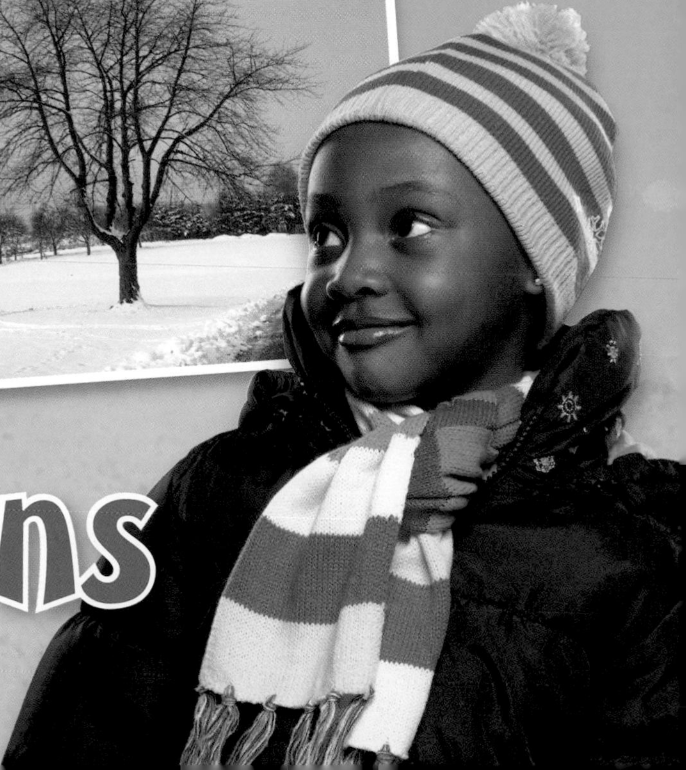

Our Seasons

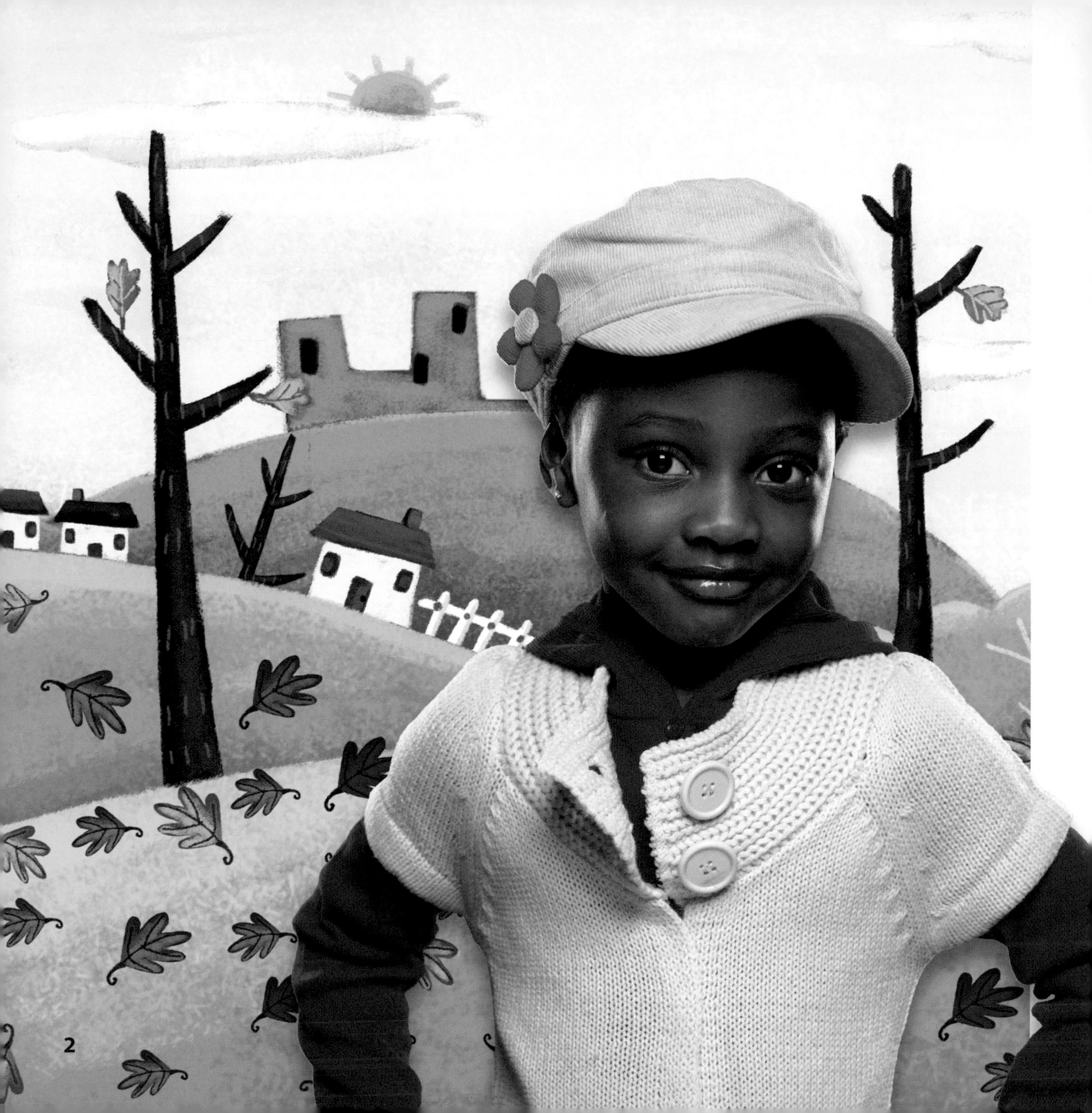

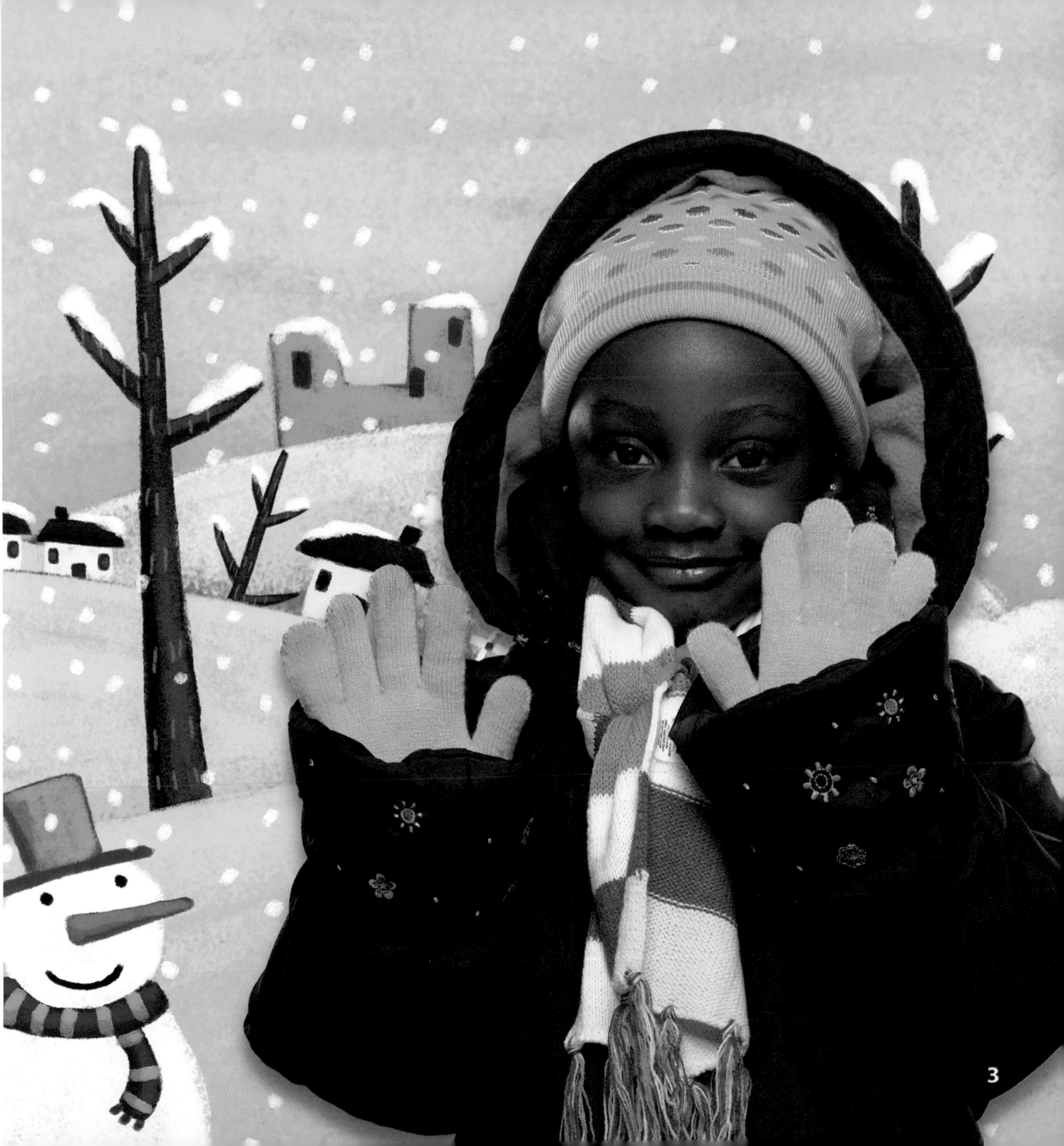

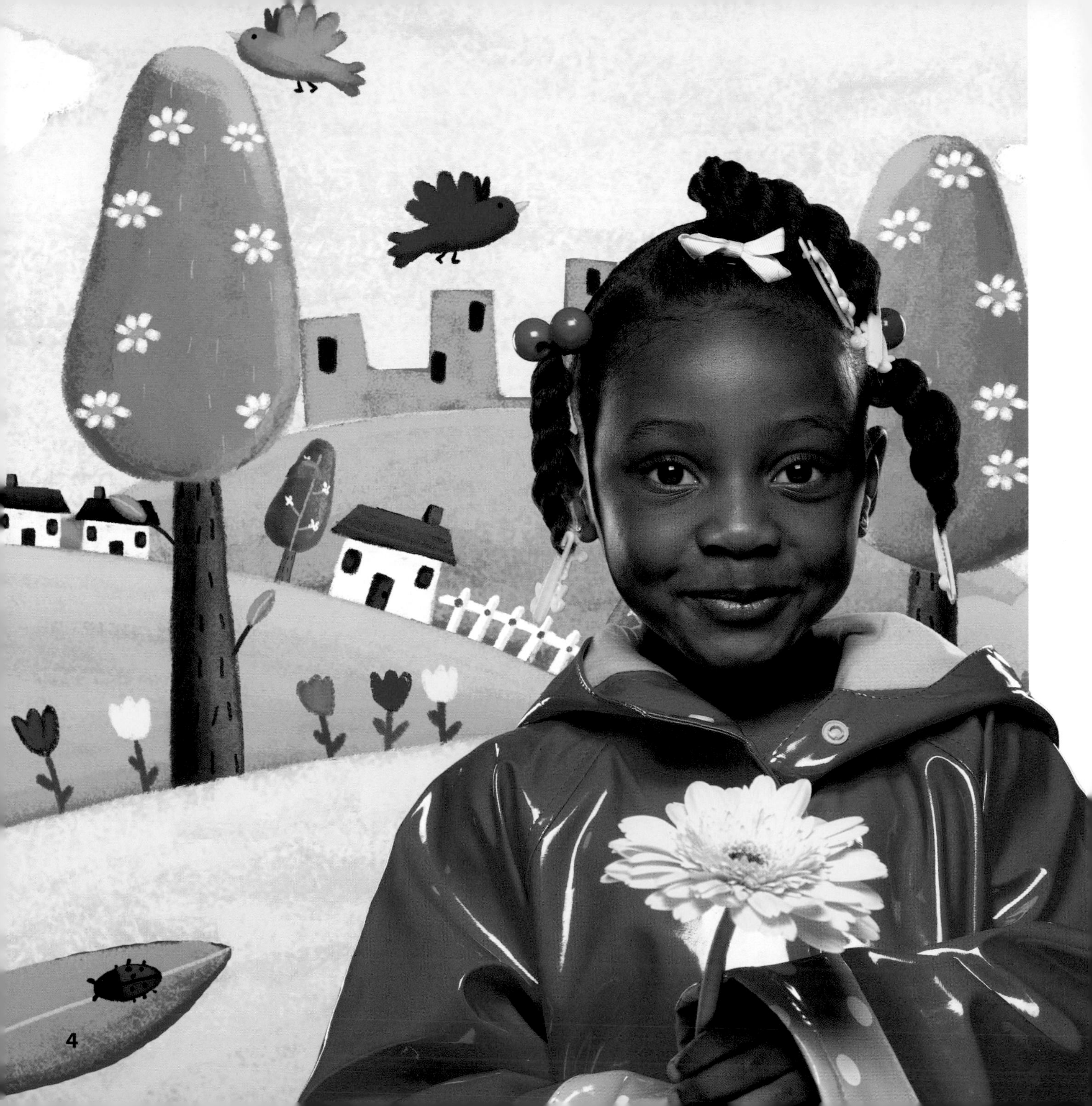

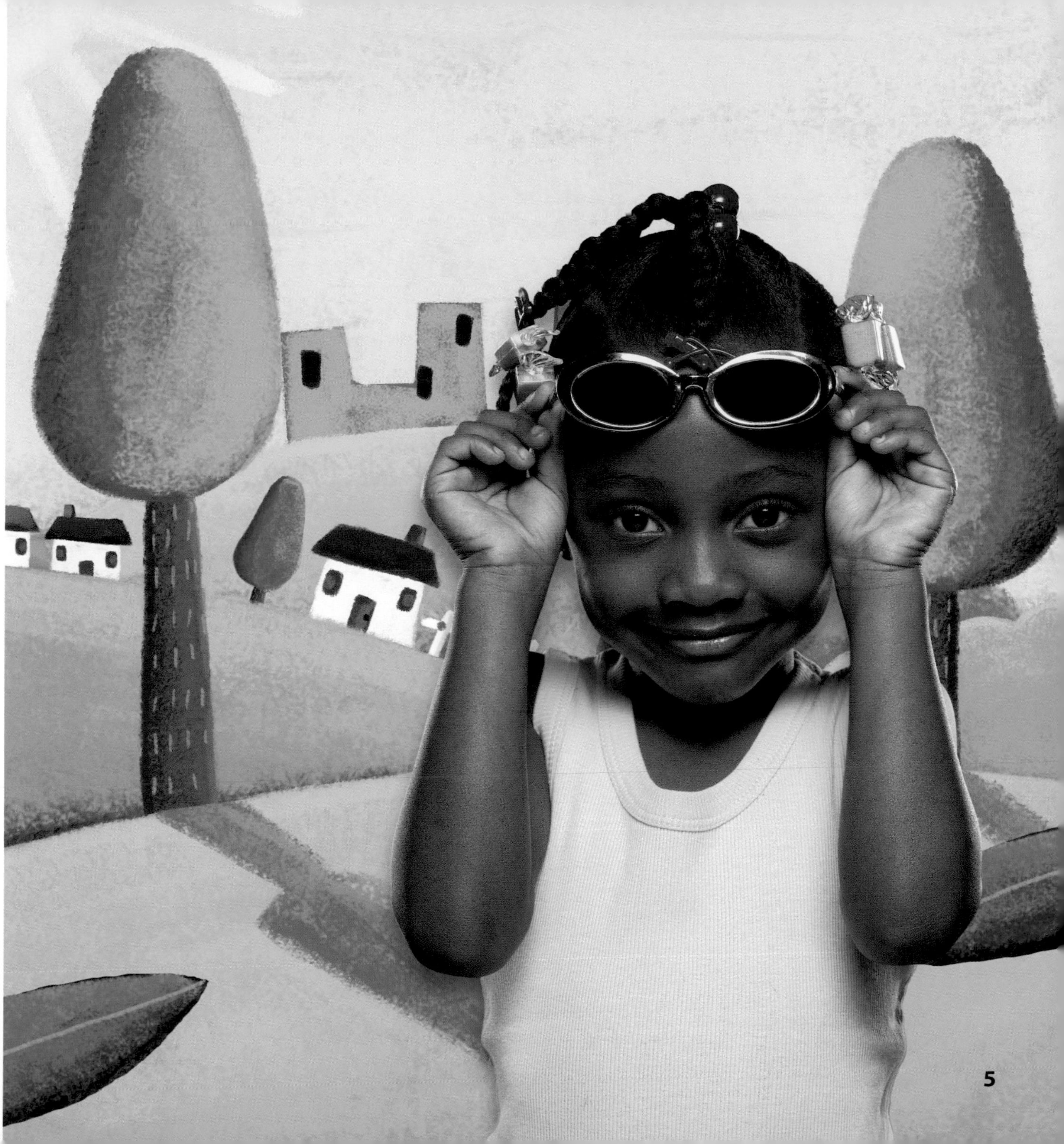

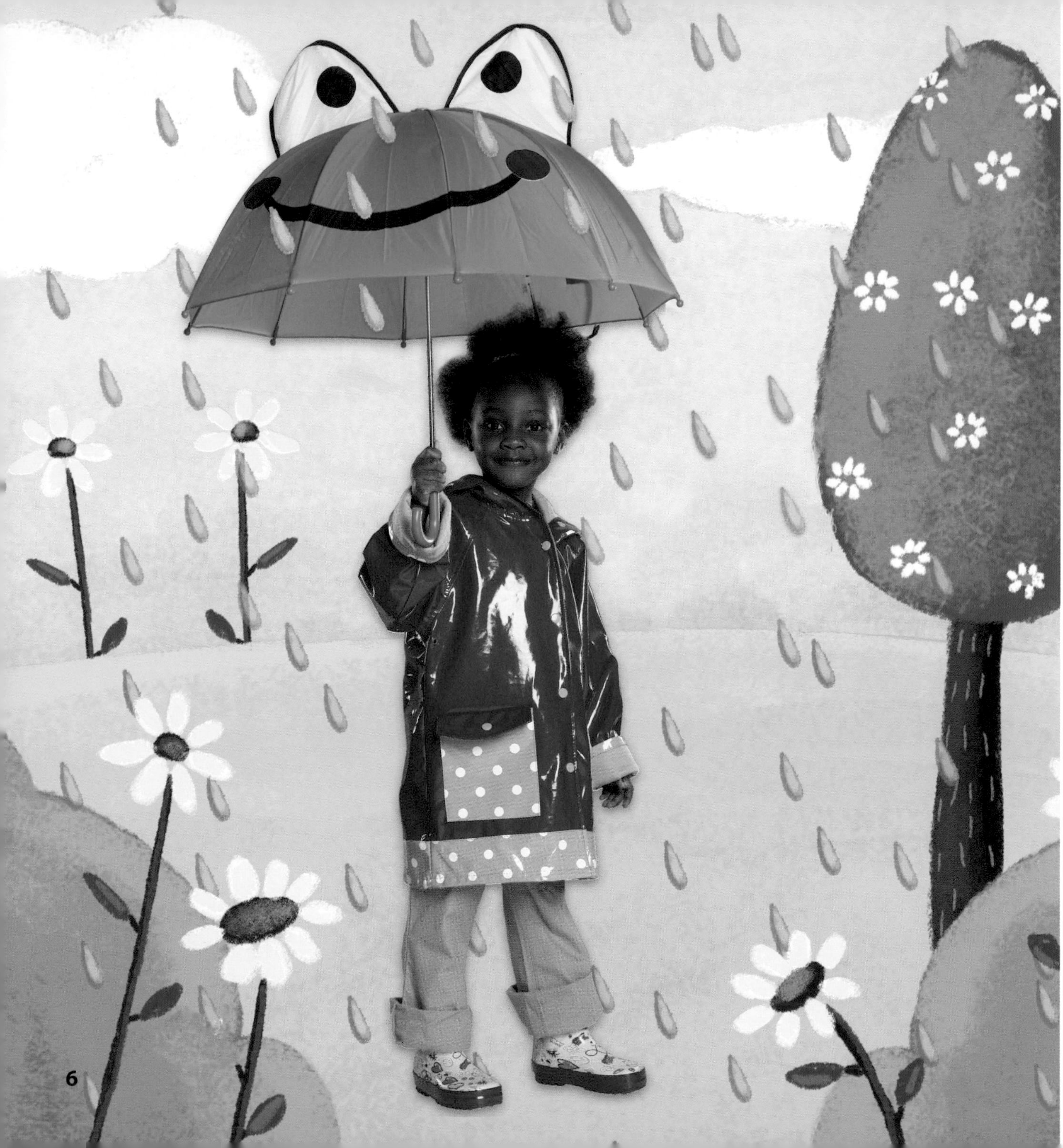

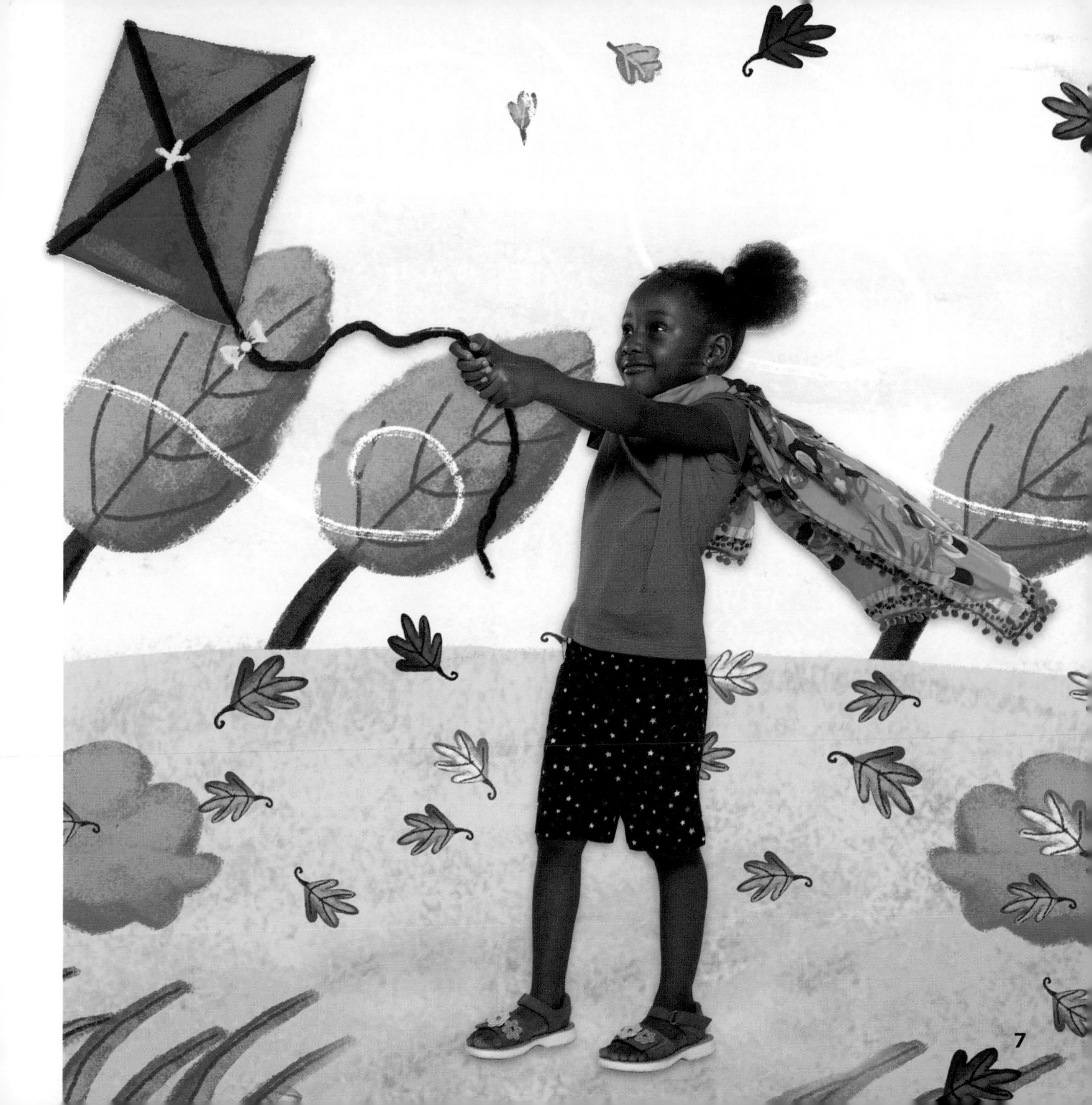

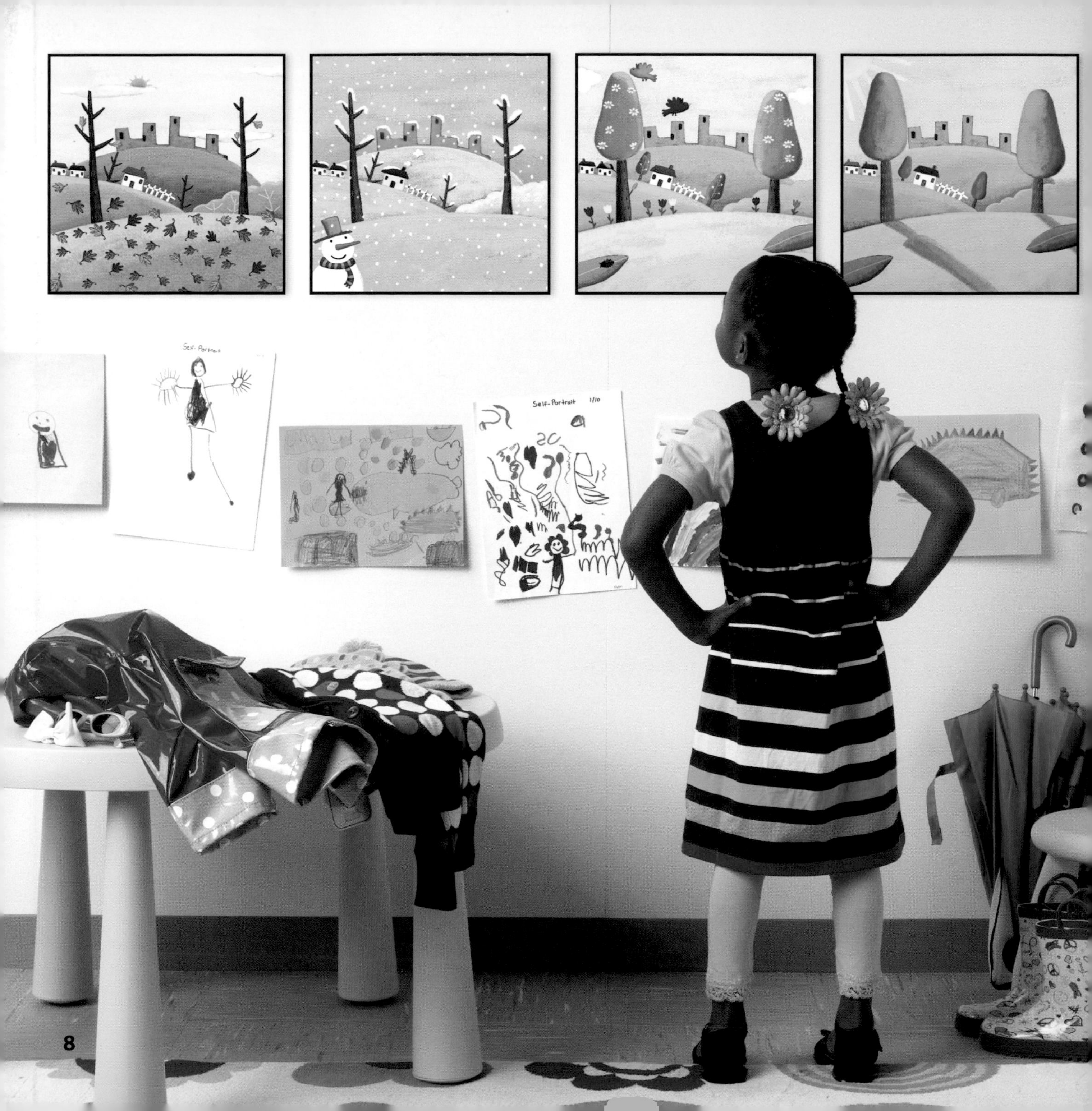
Self-Portrait
Self-Portrait 1/10